Flowers

By Gemma McMullen

Contents

©2016
Book Life
King's Lynn
Norfolk PE30 4LS

ISBN: 978-1-910512-51-7

Written by
Gemma McMullen

Edited by
Amy Allatson

Designed by
Ian McMullen

Words that appear like *this* can be
found in the glossary on page 24.

What is a Plant?

A plant is a living thing. Trees, shrubs, flowers and weeds are all plants. People and animals need plants to live.

A Plant

4

sunlight

Plants need water, sunlight and heat to live. They make their own food using energy from the sun.

What is a Flower?

Flower

All plants have different parts. A flower is part of a plant.
Not all plants have flowers.

Some flowers are large and easy to see. Some flowers are smaller. Most flowers are very pretty and smell nice.

A Sunflower is large.

A Forget-me-not is small.

7

What do Flowers look Like?

There are lots of types of flowers and they all look different. Most flowers are bright and colourful.

Daisies are *common* flowers. They can be found in gardens and fields.

Thorns

Daisy

Roses grow on bushes that have thorns to protect them.

9

What does a Flower Do?

Flowers are bright and colourful so that insects will land on them. The insects help the flowers to share their *pollen* with other flowers.

Pollen

Bees visit flowers to feed. Pollen sticks to their bodies and falls off on the next flower they visit.

Pollen

Once a flower has taken in pollen from another flower, it can make seeds. The seeds are needed for new plants to grow.

Seeds

The sunflower is made up of lots of tiny flowers which all turn into seeds.

Sunflower Seeds

Tiny Flowers

Apple Seeds

Sometimes seeds are inside fruit.

How do People use Flowers?

Flowers are very nice to look at. Many people like to keep flowers in a vase of water in their homes.

In the Home

Perfume

Some flowers smell so nice that they are used to make perfume.

Some flowers are edible, which means they can be eaten.

Broccoli is a flower!

15